WHAT WOMEN WANT

WHAT WOMEN WANT

A SELF-HELP BOOK FOR MEN
WHO DO NOT UNDERSTAND THE
PERSON THEY ARE IN A RELATIONSHIP

WITH

By

DR. GRACIETA M. LEWIS

To order additional copies of this book, contact:
Xlibris Corporation
1-888-795-4274
www.Xlibris.com
Orders@Xlibris.com
121836

Table of Contents

Acknowledgment

I would like to dedicate this book to all the men who say they do not understand women. That includes my brothers, my sons, my in laws, my fiance, and any male figures that I have come in contact with in past years. I say thank you to the men in this book who's identity has been changed to protect them. I thank them because they allowed me to have a story to tell. They allowed me to watch their actions and talk about them. I would also like to thank the women in this self-help book for allowing me to see them in their raw form and be able to talk about it and learn from it. This book was not written to disgrace any of it's characters. Instead it is being used to bless them and to promote their well being as well as tell their story. I would also like to thank my daughter for giving me the courage to produce this piece. This book is the result of a poem book that she authored, but I edited and put it in its original form. She is a bright and experienced girl in the writing of her poems. Hopefully, by the time I finish this book she would have given me some poems to add to this piece. I also want to thank my sister for her contributions. I want to also acknowledge Kim who allows me to pour out my feelings on her. She should be my therapist. And I should pay her for allowing me to pour out my guts in her ears. And I want to thank her husband for loving her and allowing her to talk to me even when it was his time to be with her.

And finally, I thank God for my grand kids. They also gave me the courage to take the time and write this piece. I also want to thank Mary Jarvis, the publisher for calling me that hot day. If she had not called I would probably not be finishing up this piece or revamping Nikki's poem book. So thank you Mary! Speaking of Mary. She is my daughter-in-law and I want to thank her too.

Preface

This piece was written as a self-help book for men. It is designed to discuss what women want. That is what they want from men and the relationships that they form. For too long men have said that they do not understand women. Well this book is designed to help men plain and simply understand what they are dealing with. They need to know what woman want. And we know that woman really do want to be understood because it benefits them. And of course when something benefits them they will do their best to find out what it is and get it. I am hoping that men will say at the end of this simple, quick read book that I have learned something. I provided pages in the book where you can jot down notes. Little tidbits to remember what you men have read. You will thank me for that space later. I also wanted this book to be as plain and as simple a possible. I hope that I accomplished just that. You can email me with your thoughts about this book at lgracieta@yahoo.com. Your feedback will be appreciated.

I want women to buy this book too. And the reason is if your husband does not purchase this book himself you buy it for him and give it to him as a present. You know you want him to understand you. And sometimes you cannot tell him in words what you need and want and desire to have. This little book will do that for you. It will put in words things you have been trying to articulate to him for years, but maybe you did not have the words to say what you needed to say. Hopefully I have done just that.

Introduction

Men talk about women all the time. Men are puzzled by the actions of women all the time. Men ask themselves questions about women that they cannot answer. What do women want? I am a man and I was created to have a women on my side to help me. Actually she (woman) is suppose to be the man's helpmate. What does a helpmate do or want? A helpmate wants to be in charge. She just does not want to help, she wants to run things. She wants to be in charge. She wants to be his boss. And many women in this day and age are the bosses of their mates. Even if women are literally the boss over men is that all they want? Okay so lets get back personally to you. Is it enough for your wife to be your boss? Is it enough for her to be the boss over your and her house. You say no! Why because you heard she wants to be over your pets; your kids, your friends; what you wear; where you go; what you eat; what you watch on t.v.; where you work; where you live and what you do! Let us not forget that she wants to control who you talk to and the number one thing is she wants to control how you spend your hard earned money. Is that okay with you? I am not trying to cause any problems between you two. I am just trying to get to the bottom of this. I just want you guys to understand one another. And the only way that's going to happen if you both put it all out on the table for the world to say "oh okay I see what's going on." And maybe you both can get the feedback you need. I am sure we needed to put this stuff out there so that once men can stop complaining about the fact that they don't know what women want. Also men are still saying they do not understand women. Not even the woman in your house. In your bed!

Sit back and let me talk to you for a little while. There are some things that I am going to say that you do not agree with me. And that's okay. I am just hoping and wishing two things. Number one, I am hoping you keep reading. Number two, I hope by your continual read of these notes you might begin to get a clearer picture of who you are living with; who you are spending your time with; and who you are trying to understand. Let's get started!

>>>>>>>>>>>>>>>>>>>>>>>NOTES>>>>>>>>>>>>>>>>>>>>>>>>

Chapter One

Did I tell you that almost every women wants someone's else man or husband if she does not have her own. Well maybe I did not because I was trying to take your feelings in account. But I realized since I was writing this that you would want me to be as honest with you as you would be with me, so here it is! How are you treating her? Are you all she wants or needs, or am I just trying to start trouble. I know this girl and I will not mention her name. She was use to being married but divorced twice, two husbands in her life. And she met this man well we will just call him Lewis. Lewis had by now been married to several women and the last marriage was about sixteen years. She was introduced to him by a relative. He looked good to her and she was interested. She knew he was married and she had failed in two marriages. Lewis told her that after sixteen years his wife, we will call her Cathy. Cathy told him that she did not want to have any sex with him. Cathy told her husband of sixteen years that she was going through menopause and that he should go and drill a hole in a pole and fuck it. Sorry for the language, but we are grownups. Just trying to be real here. I would have never told my husband to do that. And I would not have just called him a handy man. Cathy actually called her husband a handy man. The person she told this information to was both shocked and surprise. I find it difficult, however, to believe that a woman who loves her husband would discuss him in such a matter; and would talk to him the way that Cathy did. I would have paid money to be a fly on the wall when she said that pole business to her husband. And of course I did not mention that I took advantage of the situation and ended up in a hotel room. I did not "F" him, but I did make love to him at least more than once. Was it wrong of me to take advantage of the situation. I think there are those who will say it was, and those who will say it was not. Now when I think of it I should have not done it, but I did. I also went to the hotel with Lewis on many occasions. I was seen riding in his car. And I was seen at the hotel. I heard that pictures or a picture was taken. And I use to stand on corners waiting to be picked up by him. I stood out on these corners after leaving church and listening to messages from the pastor on fornication and adultery. But I did it anyway. I also dated Cathy's husband for at least nine years. I was waiting for him to leave Cathy and be with me, but things just dragged on for all of these years. Presently, he is suppose to be getting a divorce. But divorce has been stopped. Let me tell you why. In May, 2012 he was suppose to be too sick to make it to court, so the judge rescheduled the case to August 10, 2012. This time he was in the hospital due to some blood work. Lewis thought he had cancer. I thought he had cancer. I told him that he needed to leave his situation and come and let me take care of him. Lewis heard what I said, but he did not call me for about a week. So, I did not know if he was dying or whether or not he made it to the divorce court. I found out later, a week later that he was not working at the same location for two weeks, never made it to court, and was released out of the hospital. So when I did talk to him I gave him a date that he should be divorced and ready to move. I am sorry, but I cannot give you that date. But, it may have already come and gone by the time this book gets printed. Lewis told me he needed six weeks to get his teeth done before he could go anywhere. I was startled.

>>>>>>>>>>>>>>>>>>>>>>NOTES>>>>>>>>>>>>>>>>>>>>>>>>>

Chapter Two

Let's talk about what I said in the introduction of this piece. You know this is just a piece of information. I want you to never question yourself again where it pertains to women. I want you to know with out a doubt what you are dealing with. You deserve to know. You do not need to be second guessing her. You need to be sure about what you are doing. And the only way to do that is for you to be sure of what she is saying to you. You need to be sure that you are understanding exactly what you are hearing. You know how sometime you hear someone talking but you are not sure of what she is saying. Well this has gone on for too long. It frustrates men when they talk to women about different things pertaining to them personally and they can not make sense of what is coming out of their mouth. That needs to stop. When you finish reading this piece of information, you at least will say "Wow at least now I have a better understanding of what she wants." And maybe that will make you and her happier in the bed and in your relationship. Well we will see! We were talking about the man's helpmate, the woman. Besides your helpmate is suppose to help you. Can you say today that your mate helps you. Let's be honest. Answer these questions truthfully. Does she help you with the day to day chores? No, she just does the bare minimum. Does she pay some of the bills. No she just spends her money on her self. She buys dresses. She buys shoes. She buys earrings. She buys undies and night gowns to fit her taste, not yours. Does she drive the kids to school. Yes, only if she is not tied up with her own agenda and schedule for the day. Does she run your errands too. No, because she is too caught up doing her own thing. But what happen to this helpmate? She is still there hidden behind a mask of faithfulness and fullness toward herself. She wants to fulfill her purpose and her dreams. And those dreams may or may not line up with yours. For example, if you two buy a house together. Who makes the final decision on what type of house it is? She does. Who makes the final decision on what type of furniture goes into the house. She does. Who decides on who sleeps in what room. She does. Forget all that, who decides on where your new address is? She does. And who decides when you all move. And of course the answer is she does cause you are too busy doing other things. At least that is her excuse to you and the world for taking over. But listen this is simply your helpmate. The helpmate you use to swear by, but now you are only sure of one thing. She wants to be the boss over me. That's what she wants. I am sure of it. It's clearer than the sky. It's clearer than this half filled glass of water. You are wrong nothing is that clear with her. Because, if you complain about what she is doing, she will say "Honey I am only trying to help." And you will say "Okay honey I appreciate what you are doing. I love you for it and please keep up the good work." You just signed and dotted on the line your contract for her being the boss. You just gave her the okay to continue what she is doing to you. You just gave her your stamp of approval. You say no you did not. Where were you? I and the world say "Yes you did." Okay well we nipped that in the bud, so let us move on to some more important things. Some things that have been bugging you for the longest. The kids.

>>>>>>>>>>>>>>>>>>>>>>NOTES>>>>>>>>>>>>>>>>>>>>>>

Chapter Three

Who do the kids look like? Are they all you or are they all her? What do the people in and out of your family say they look like? Does she smile when they say that the kids look like her? Or is she sadden when there are those who say that the kids look like you? You do not pay that mush attention right. Then maybe you should. I tell you what for argument purposes and to save face let's just say she may crack a smile off the side of her face when people say the kids look like you. But I assure you she's going to fix that dilemma. What does she do? Well Mincy will just take the kids to the department store and buy the kids clothes she thinks they should wear. Without your help or without your approval. Docs Mincy take pictures of the kids outfits with her camera phone and send them to Chris. Maybe! Maybe not! If Mincy does what message do Chris send her back. He says "Honey that looks nice." And in fact Chris just says "Go ahead and keep making the kids dress like Mincy wants them to look and Chris just said okay I approve. The question is why did he say okay I approve. I will tell you why. Because Chris just does not want to start an argument. So, for the sake of arguing Chris agrees to the kiddie take over. Chris did not even question the cost. He was simply satisfied and happy he did not have to take the brats shopping. Cause Chris hates to even go shopping for groceries with the kids. He hates the way the kids act in the store. Chris does not want to be alone with the kids in public, because he is scared of how they are going to act. So Chris avoids any activities where Mincy is not with him and the kids. Mincy does not tell Chris she keeps the tags on the clothing so she can take the clothes back in a week and get her money back. I wonder what Chris would say about that if he knew. Let me answer that for you. Chris would probably say nothing because for the sake of argument he wants to keep the peace. At least Chris thinks he is keeping the peace. He is simply just digging a larger hole for himself. Does Chris truly not know what he is doing? No he does not. You see Chris is willing to do whatever it takes to keep Mincy from going off on him. Chris is trying to keep the status quo. Can you blame him? No and yes! Chris will not admit it but he is afraid of Mincy. And so its what Mincy says, what Mincy wants, and what Mincy does is fine with Chris. What a one-sided household. Can you imagine living in that madness everyday, 24-7 and on weekends. I can not, but I know who did.

>>>>>>>>>>>>>>>>>>>>>>NOTES>>>>>>>>>>>>>>>>>>>>>>>>

Chapter Four

Lets go back for a moment and bring up Cathy and Lewis again. Lewis finally filed for divorce after sixteen years of marriage. Lewis was finally tired of being bullied. He was finally tired of being told what to do; where to go and how to think. But that was not good enough. Cathy monitored his phone calls. Cathy cooked Lewis food and made sure he ate what she wanted him to eat. She monitored his mail. And moved his things around. For example, Lewis would place an important document on the desk. When he went back to get it it would have been removed by Cathy. She removed his court appointment. He had to call the court and ask for another appointment slip. She did not want him, but she told him she would not give him a divorce because she knew he had another woman. That's what women want. They only want the man if somebody else wants him. This was the case with Cathy. Cathy had a picture of his lover, and she showed it to the judge. Cathy hoped that the judge would rule that Lewis could not get a divorce because he was seeing another woman. That woman was me and that was a picture of Lewis and I going into a hotel like I said earlier. Cathy had Lewis's back up against the wall. She was in total control of his destiny. Lewis had to admit to the judge and Cathy that yes he did enter a hotel room with me, he did make love to me, and he was in fact in love with me. Cathy had her answer, but it just made her wanting to control the situation somehow. Cathy even used their daughter as her attorney until her daughter decided that she could not represent her mother against her father. So Cathy retained the same lawyer Lewis had. Again she's attempting to control the court, control the lawyer and control Lewis. They had to go to court appointed marriage counselors. In these meetings with the marriage counselors, Cathy would see and talk to one and Lewis would talk to another one. Then they would switch and talk to the other marriage counselor. Cathy told the marriage counselor everything except she was not having sex with Lewis. It was not until Lewis told his marriage counselor that his wife was not having sex with him did the sex issue come out. You see having sex or not having sex with your mate is a way of controlling the relationship and the intimacy between a man and a woman. It also causes the man to look outside of the house for sex. And when he finds it he goes crazy if its good. And then he refuses to touch his wife even though the marriage counselor instructs him to. She gets some instructions too. And she tries to seal her end of the deal by showing up to bed naked trying to tempt Lewis into having sex with her. Does Lewis give in? Would not you and I want to know for sure. Lewis says he did not. But can one really be sure. Of course not. Now the control still goes back to Cathy who now controls how I think. Cathy says she will never give up her husband. That's been true so far cause she went to the court and told the judge that Lewis did not want a divorce. There's that wanting to be in control of another person's life again. It is as clear as day. Don't you see it? It's what women want!

>>>>>>>>>>>>>>>>>>>>>>>NOTES>>>>>>>>>>>>>>>>>>>>>>>

Chapter Five

So then we can say that I want what she has. I want her husband. And that is the truth. If I did not want him I would not have hung in it with Lewis for nine going on ten years. Even though I almost got caught with him on several occasions. And if I could not have him all to myself then I would share Lewis with Cathy. I at least had some part of him that I was in control of. And she had a piece of control too. But you see Cathy had the largest part. She slept in his bed every night. She had his company everyday and every night. She cooked his food and they ate together. Cathy even washed his clothes, folded them and tucked them away. She even had his child. A girl to look, act and dress like her. Cathy also drove in his car. He was not allowed to go to the store alone. He did not use the computer. She monitored all the phone calls, the bills and all the bank accounts. She knew what was in the accounts and she took money out of his account and transferred money to her account. She bought some of his clothes and dressed him like she wanted him to look. Cathy went out to eat with Lewis to restaurants as his wife. He had no time to himself. She, Cathy that is was in control. She was and has been right where she wants to be controlling his life. Oh, did I mention that they take trips together. They have gone to Disney world in Orlando several times. And they have gone to other places. She tries to get him to go to church with her but he will not. But she keeps pressuring him to go to pastoral meetings and events at her church. Sometimes he goes and that's what she wants. While she is in church he calls me and talks with me until 1:30 p.m. or if I am in town we meet after church usually about 11:30 a.m. and go to the hotel. We stay at the hotel for about two hours and I get dropped off around the corner from my house, so I walk home and go in the house like nothing happened.

>>>>>>>>>>>>>>>>>>>>>>NOTES>>>>>>>>>>>>>>>>>>>>>>>>

Chapter Six

I know this girl lets call her Susan. She was working with Stewart. Stewart was married. Stewart's wife asked Susan to move in until she got another job. Susan agreed. When Susan moved in she wanted my room, so I gave it to her. That was not all she wanted. She wanted Stewart. How do I know it. She worked with Stewart. She would talk to Stewart for hours about his personal life. That usually included his wife and the kids. Susan wanted to keep Mary's kids. She did not have any kids of her own. She did not have a husband of her own, so she wanted Mary's husband. One day they were all in the garage talking and Susan was wearing a dress. She was talking to Stewart and Mary. She kept pulling up her dress and getting closer to Stewart. I had to tell her to put her dress down. She was about to show Stewart her private parts. She seemed like she was in a daze. She simply wanted Stewart. A husband of her own. When it did not seem like she was getting to Stewart fast enough her attention turned to Mary. Susan knew what she wanted. I confronted Susan and Susan wanted me out of the house. So, she told Stewart that I approached her in a bad manner. Stewart immediately took her side and approached me in a negative manner. Stewart wanted me out of the house. Where was I to go? Stewart told Mary and Mary told me I would have to leave and go somewhere. I told Mary that I had no where to go. Mary said I had no choice but to go some place. Susan was happy because she was getting her way. I was told to go to Miami. I told Mary that I could not live in Miami. So I did not go to Miami, but I was told I had to go somewhere. I chose to go to Savannah, Georgia where my brother lives. I figure that was a safer place.

I was later found to be wrong, but first I felt that I would be safe. Maybe I will tell you about Savannah in this piece, or the next piece I write about. We will see and you will too. After I had decided to leave they did not want me to go. They said I needed to stay, so Mary and Susan asked me to stay. I said nothing, but then Susan apologized and said she was sorry. She said all that to get what she wanted. And what she wanted was for me to stay and not leave. So I did! It's funny how the tears and the apologies will come forth when a woman wants something. Whether the apologies are real or false they always come forth to win approval and to get one's way. And it works. At least in this case it does. So I stayed! And I got my room back. All that was done to keep me in the house. It's amazing what Mary and Susan would go through to get their way. But once again what a woman wants a woman gets. Susan got what she wanted, so she started working on the kids. Susan started giving Mary's daughter clothing. Why I do not know. The only thing I could think she wanted something from her. Maybe loyalty. Why loyalty? Because loyalty led to getting something else. Susan and I fought over my grand kids. She wanted to run the show when it came to her and the smallest child named Bradley. Bradley was a little guy and Susan wanted to control what he did and thought. Susan thought she could teach Bradley things better than I could. Now listen I was the teacher for many years. I had attained all the degrees, but Susan felt she was better at the game of kids. She wanted Mary's kids. Why did she want Mary's kids. Maybe because she did not have her own and she wanted Mary's and Stewart's kids. Just what a woman wants. She sees it and sets her sight on it and then goes in for the kill. That's just how a woman works. She's just like an attack dog after a piece of meat. As long as the meat is not around she does not want it. But as soon as the meat is displayed she wants what she sees and the get what you want mode kicks in. Wow, this is what a woman wants.

>>>>>>>>>>>>>>>>>>>>>>NOTES>>>>>>>>>>>>>>>>>>>>>>>

Chapter Seven

Remember we are talking about what women want. Well let us get down to the low down. A woman wants to feel loved and cherished. She wants to feel loved in all of her relationships. She wants to feel cherished. Cherished by her kids, by her mate and by her acquaintances. She wants to feel secure and safe. Secure in her relationships. The ones she initiates and the ones she just walks into. It's like wearing a slip up under her dress. She wants to feel that that slip is not going to hang from under her dress. because if it does, then her underclothes via her slip will be exposed. Just think does a woman ever want her underwear to be revealed. I say for the sake of an argument, yes. When it suits her needs and gets her what she wants she will walk the street with no undies on. And she's not scared to reveal just that. what do men think about it. They think its great. They look at the high skirt and lifted dress with a stamp of approval. They just want to get what they can get and see what they can see. Just revealing a little bit about what the man wants too. She gives it all to get it all. She places it all on the line to get the line in return. She is woman and that is just what she does. Oh, another thing. She is not afraid to prove her womanhood. Cause she knows when she proves herself it just gets her closer to what she wants. And of course she gets what she wants. She is a receiver. That means she gets things. She receives his love. She receives his money. She receives his sperm. She receives his kids. She receives his home. She receives his mail. She receives his information. Why does she receive things. She receives things because she's built that way. Men are givers. They give a woman what she wants. But she helps him give it to her by receiving it. Just like I said that's how she is made. She is woman or wow man. Wow man you are out for the run of your life. She is going to nag you, bug you, bother you, irritate you, manipulate you in a need to get what she wants. And guess what you let her. Why do you do this? I got an answer for you. You are just trying to keep the peace. You are trying to keep confrontation down. You are trying to please her. And that is what she wants. And she's willing to fight for what she wants. It does not matter the means. Because the means produces the results. And the results is what she wants. She does not want to loose. She wants to win. And win she does at the game of life. At any cost. The cost is never too much. It's the results that make it all worth it. That's just what a woman wants. And she expects you (man) to give her what she wants or else. Or else what. Or else you are not going to be happy. You will not have any peace or satisfaction. You will catch hell and not know how to get out of it unless you give her what she wants. That's the bottom line. I cannot make it any clearer than that. Can you at least get a better picture of what you are dealing with. I sure hope so, because this piece was written to help you out. Am I at least doing that?

>>>>>>>>>>>>>>>>>>>>>>>NOTES>>>>>>>>>>>>>>>>>>>>>>>>

Chapter Eight

So let's keep it personal. Lewis had not called me for at least a week, but it feels longer. I want and I need to hear from him. I feel like calling his house and asking him what is his problem. And I suppose if she did not go to church she may be home and she may get an unexpected phone call from her husband's woman. And why is that? It is because I am tired of being in the dark. I need to need to know and I want to know what's going on. I do not understand him and why he will not call. Sometimes when a man does not call that speaks volumes. So what should I do. I call his friend almost everyday and tells him to tell Lewis to call me because I want to hear from him. I want him to reconfirm his love and devotion. I need and want to feel secure in our relationship. I almost do not care if calling his private home phone number is crossing the line. I am tired of being ignored. It's getting on my nerve. I do not deserve to be treated this way. A phone call goes a long way. And when you do not get it it makes a woman furious. I want what I want. And that's a phone call. Is that asking too much? Am I being unreasonable? I do not think so! Well I called and I did get plenty of answers. Lewis is not sick. He does not have cancer. Lewis does not have his phone any more because it was too expensive, so he can not call anyone. And yes Lewis is working in a different building, so he could not even use his friend's phone. And no Lewis is not even taking breaks or eating lunch. He says its because he is behind schedule. And finally, Lewis has to move out of his house because the bank is taking the house. Or, hopefully the lawyer has found someone to buy the house. What a woman wants is what a woman gets and that's answers. It took courage to call, but that is what a woman is willing to do and willing to go to get what she wants. Do women take chances to get what they want. Of course they do. What would I have done if Cathy had answered the phone. I would have hung up. And that would have been the wrong thing to do. My friend told me that in that case if Cathy answered the phone then I should have asked for someone, preferably a woman. I did not think of that. If I had hung up, then Cathy would have called back and if I had not answered the phone she would have heard the voice mail. Then I would have been found out, so I changed the voice mail to reflect just the phone number and no name. You see she knows about me in the back of her mind, but I cannot let myself come to the forefront. That's not what I want. What I want is to get Lewis and then I will come to the forefront. I will not care what Cathy knows or what she thinks.

>>>>>>>>>>>>>>>>>>>>>NOTES>>>>>>>>>>>>>>>>>>>>>>>>

Chapter Nine

Women do not talk to other women. That is because unless it benefits her she is not about to spill her guts. But if it does benefit her somehow then guts she will spill. Women would rather talk to men than their own gender. That is that way because women do not trust women. I mean if a woman is going to speak to a psych doctor that doctor should be a male not a female. Why is it easier to talk to a male doctor rather than a female doctor. Because the male doctor listens eagerly and offers feedback that is practical and easier to complete. Female psych doctors offer very little feedback. Female psych doctors are often quicker to hospitalize you than male doctors. Male doctors understand a statement better and are not quick to come to a negative conclusion. But a female psych doctor is patient and listens quietly to his patients/clients. Then after he has heard what his patient has said he is willing to offer his feedback. And I must say the feedback is clear and practical. Male psych doctors leave you with something that you can do. A practical application to a spoken truth. That's what the female client needs and wants. I recall a time that Cindy was diagnosed as having a mental problem and needed to be sent to a psych ward. She acted out at home and was transferred to a treatment facility. It was her mother who called the therapist who happened to be male. He called and had her transported via police car to a treatment facility. When Cindy got to the facility the police took her through the front door. While Cindy was going to the front door she started asking for Paul. She was calling his name at the top of her lungs. He was not there. And mentally it seems like Cindy was not there either. It seemed that Cindy's mind had been transported some where else. Could that be possible. Maybe Cindy's shell of a body was there, but her soul was some where else. I do not even know how that is possible. While in the care of the mental treatment facility, Cindy made weird statements throughout the day and night. Who was she talking to. She was talking to someone in her head. At least it seemed that way. But then it sounded like someone was in the room, so she was talking to them. How can you hold a conversation in your head. Is it possible? Yes it is! You can have all sort of conversations in your mind without even verbally answering back. But what happens when you really start answering back. If Cindy talks back to herself, then what happens next? Cindy is admitted into the treatment center in order to spend some time being monitored and being interrogated, so she thought! Cindy said that's what they did to her. She talked and they listened. What she said was a direct result of them questioning her. The doctor said welcome to hell. Why would he say something like that? Who was he talking to? Was he talking to her body or her soul? It seemed like he was talking to her soul, because her body was in bad shape. But how can her body be on earth and her soul be gone? That just does not make any sense. If her body is on earth and her soul is gone, then why is she still alive and well. That is the dilemma she and every other woman faces. The answers that go unanswered. At least for now. That's not what she wants, but that is what Cindy gets.

>>>>>>>>>>>>>>>>>>>>>>>>NOTES>>>>>>>>>>>>>>>>>>>>>>>>

Chapter Ten

I may get off the subject for a moment, but I want to know how can a man be alive when his soul is missing in action. Does his soul go to hell or heaven? And does his body wait around to go to the dust of the ground where it originated from or what? Did he steal someone else's soul? Or, did he get a reprieve some how? I just do not know the answer to this question. Let us just say for the sake of an argument that he stole someone else's soul. How did he do it? How did he or she do it? How much more time does it give him or her on earth? I am really wondering about this while I am sitting outside in the cool of the day. While the breeze is blowing cool air my way. It's still hot as hell outside and the loud sound of cars starting up and driving off do not help. There is no manuscript written on this sorted subject matter. Where does the soul go and how long can it stay there without the spirit and the body. You see I want answers to these questions. All I can do is tell you what it feels like. I think I can express some of the details. Maybe these details can shine a new light on the subject matter. The soul leaves the body and travels to places unknown. The soul hears people talking like there are right in the place where he or she is. I suppose the soul is both male or female depending on the gender of the body. Does that make sense? What are they saying? They are threating the soul with words like we got her and she is dead. A full fledge conversation is going on between the persons and the soul. Or between the interrogator's souls and the soul of the person being questioned. When is the best time to question the soul of the person? The best time is when he or she is between sleep and awake.

It is during that time that the person is sleep and wake at the same time. It's almost like being hypnotized. And if the person is on medication or some drug at the time that makes the psychotic episodes more serious. But no one wants to talk about these events until now. And why now is because the truth needs to come out, and this is what the patient/client wants. Are these hallucinations for real or are they simply imagined. Were these dreams or misplaced emotional episodes. I do not know! But, I want to know. That's why I am searching for answers. it's the need and the want to know that's pushing me forward.

>>>>>>>>>>>>>>>>>>>>>>NOTES>>>>>>>>>>>>>>>>>>>>>>>

Chapter Eleven

I know this girl named Stephanie. Stephanie was married to Richard. Richard was having an affair with other women. Richard lived in another city while Stephanie lived in another city. Living in separate houses and cities was due to their working conditions. Richard took advantage of the separation and hoe hopped on his wife. Why did Richard do it because he could. Richard got his way because he was not living with Stephanie and his kids. Richard did what Richard wanted to do because he was left alone in his own devices. Richard came to see Stephanie and his kids on some weekends. And Stephanie would go to see him on weekends. Finally Richard divorced Stephanie. Stephanie paid Richard alimony. It was a large sum of money, so I heard. He broke Stephanie's heart. She could and had to believe that some other woman wanted her husband. And she (the other woman) got him. But that did not stop Stephanie for wanting Richard back. Why I do not know, or maybe Stephanie just loved and was really in love with Richard. So, Stephanie and Richard got a divorce. They went their separate ways. But there was still contact between them because of the kids. The kids were angry that their father had divorced their mother. But they still loved their father. Stephanie wanted her husband back. I heard she would cry over him. Stephanie just wanted to know why she could not hold onto her husband. No one could answer that question but Richard. Stephanie got him back. Why Stephanie wanted him back I do not know because Richard did not treat Stephanie right. He did not talk to Stephanie right. But she wanted him back and she got him back. I think she got him back when she ignored him and made Richard feel like he was not so important to her. Then she turned around and did something for herself. She had her breast enlarged. She went to sleep with small breast and woke up with nice round, plump breast. Richard did not want Stephanie to get her breast enlarged. Richard did not want any other man looking at Stephanie. Stephanie looked good. From head to feet Stephanie looked good and is in great shape. She's not just turning Richard head. She's turning some other heads too. Is that what she wants. Maybe her goal is to make Richard jealous. And jealous he is. Stephanie got what she wanted. She also finally got the respect she deserved.

Woman want to look good. By looking good Stephanie felt good and that's what she wanted. She did not care how much it cost her to enlarge her breast. She got the looks she wanted. And I think that is one of the best things that could have happen to Stephanie.

>>>>>>>>>>>>>>>>>>>>>>>NOTES>>>>>>>>>>>>>>>>>>>>>>>>

Chapter Twelve

Let's get real personal. What do I as a woman want? You know the story behind Lewis and me. Well I think I have proven that I want Lewis, but there are other things that I want. I know Lilly. And Lilly is a pretty girl. She wears wigs and dresses nice. Her hair looks good and her clothing are on point. She wears long sun dresses. After seeing how great Lilly looked I wanted to look like Lilly, so I bought long sun dresses too. And I bought two wigs from Lilly. You see I wanted to look like Lilly. I also bought nice earrings to go with my outfits. It was because I wanted to be in the same category as Lilly. What was I trying to prove? I was trying to prove that I could look good too. I had to take another woman's idea of what looked good. So I stole Lilly's look and made it my own. I felt good and I looked good just like Lilly. I still have those dresses. And I bought two more wigs. And I bought some more dresses, and earrings.

I even tried to work in the health care field. Lilly has worked in the health care field for years. So trying to be like her, I got a job in the same field. I worked for about two weeks with elderly people. I was a sitter. A sitter is like a nurses aide. I was called in to work as needed. I changed the patient's diaper. I fed the client. And I also dressed the client. I could not keep up with the work, so I was fired. And that was not what I wanted. I wanted to work because I like my own money.

>>>>>>>>>>>>>>>>>>>>>>NOTES>>>>>>>>>>>>>>>>>>>>>>>

Chapter Thirteen

Additionally, a woman wants to feel safe and secure. I may have touched on this before, but I am sure I did not go into details. A woman wants to feel safe and secure in her environment. She maybe does not drive at night because she does not feel safe. A man makes a woman feel; safe or not. That's why she wants to cuddle up with him because it makes her feel safe and loved. She does not have to have sex or make love to feel secure. She just has to have him. He makes her feel safe. That is why a woman prefers not to go anywhere by herself. She would prefer to be with her mate, him. He has the ability to make her feel safe and secure. And he has the ability to make her feel unsafe and insecure. She can also feel mentally insecure in herself. That is why woman do plastic surgery or have some other work done on herself. How she looks makes her feel safe and secure in herself. If she is fat and out of shape she may not feel mentally secure. If he's talking to her in a negative way, she may not feel secure in herself. And trust me she wants to feel mentally secure and safe. That's why woman go to therapists and psych doctors when they have an emotional problem. She needs to talk it out. She wants to straighten it out mentally. She needs to do that in order to feel secure and safe in her own being. How much she is willing to reveal to the therapists just depends on her short and long term goals. What she shares with her doctor or therapist is depended on how much she trust him. If she does not trust him totally then she will limit what she shares with him. If she does not feel mentally safe with him she may not reveal too much or just enough to feel somewhat emotionally secure. She feels that if her head is straight then her body will follow. And that's usually the case. A woman wants to feel secure and safe on the inside of herself. She feels that if she is safe and secure there then she is safe and secure outwardly. She needs and desires an encouraging word to feel secure on the inside. She needs to think right and do the right thing. She needs to walk in love and by doing that she is reaping love in return. And I mean walk in love toward her brother and her sisters. I am not talking about her other siblings, I am talking about people she comes in contact with, other humans.

When a woman receives positive input from people around her it makes her feel safe and secure. When she does not get that positive feedback it makes her feel insecure. Insecurity leads to low self esteem. And low self esteem leads to a host of other things, but mainly insecurity.

>>>>>>>>>>>>>>>>>>>>>>NOTES>>>>>>>>>>>>>>>>>>>>>>>>>

Chapter Fourteen

Let's revisit the subject of a job. I know a lady named Penny. Penny was laid off from her job for whatever reason. So, for a long time Penny did not work. Penny drew unemployment. After years of not working, Penny finally got a temporary job. When Penny got that temporary position, I wanted to get a job too. So I applied for a job at a retirement home working with the elderly. I changed the elderly person's diaper. In other words I cleaned up shit because I wanted a job. I wanted to prove myself. I wanted to prove that just like Penny I could get a job too. I also wanted to have my own money. Money to purchase what I wanted when I wanted it. There is nothing like having your own money. Having your own money makes you feel like you are in charge of your own life. And of course that's what a woman wants. She wants to feel like she is in charge. One of the ways to feel that way is to have your own. It's not enough to depend on someone else for money. Then when you need money, you have to keep going to him for money. It's bad enough having to work for someone in order to get money. It's better to be your own boss. It's better to generate your own funds. It's just better to work for yourself. So, with that thought in mind I decided to sell Avon and jewelry. I sold Avon before and did not do a good job at it. I ended up buying the Avon for myself. I'm really not a good seller. I do not know how to ask people to buy something from me. It helps with Avon to have the books. That way all you have to do is hand someone the book and ask them to call you with an order to buy something. Then you have to purchase what they want at a discount and when the merchandise comes in they pay you. And even though you get a discount, you still have to come up with the money for the merchandise. In other words you have to provide the money up front. In a further effort to have my own money and to be my own boss I have decided to get a booth at the flee market and sell jewelry. I bought some wholesale jewelry from this company online in order to make some money. As of the writing of this piece I probably have been to the flea market selling my jewelry. I will probably need to get some business cards made up. That will be one way to let people know that I am in business for myself. And trust me there is nothing like being in business for yourself. To once again be your own boss. It;s a wonderful feeling. I know because I use to own a family day care center. I kept children. The ages ranged from infant to after school kids. The government paid me for keeping the kids. They even reimbursed me for the food I was feeding the kids. I was so good at what I did that I was able to hire an employee to work with me. It felt good being in charge and having my own money and of course being my boss and the boss of someone else. Every week I had that check in my hand. It was worth it.

>>>>>>>>>>>>>>>>>>>>>NOTES>>>>>>>>>>>>>>>>>>>>>>>>>

Chapter Fifteen

I know this guy named Billy. Billy was a preacher in a church. He ministered the word on a regular basis. He was legally blind, but he could see shapes and figures. He read braille. In other words he read these huge books with his fingers. Simply put he got mad with the pastor at the church and decided to go back to school. He was angry at God I think. So, we got married and I left my job. I left my job to follow him to school. Was that the right thing to do. Probably not! I think about it now and I must say I should have retired from the job so that I could have a pension today. I do not have a pension today because I walked off from a perfectly sound job to be with a man. I wanted to be married to Billy. Well I did not follow Billy off to school at first. Billy went by himself, but he got sick and returned home. But instead of telling him it's okay to not go to school I sent him back. I told him he needed to go back to school. I told him I would go with him and help him. You see I wanted my husband to succeed. Because if he succeed then I would also. That's how I felt. And to some degree that was true. We stayed in campus housing. And I enrolled in the same program that my husband was in. You see I did not plan on going to college. I had dropped out of school because I had gotten pregnant. After I had my baby I went back and got my diploma. I never planned on going to college, but I wanted to keep my husband, so I did what he did. I went to school too. I did not know it at the beginning that this move would open up a lot of doors. My husband needed a tutor and so I became his reader. I read books on tape for him and got paid for it by the Disability department at the school.

I did that for several years and got paid for it. Then I graduated and so did he. Then he decided to pursue a master's degree. In order for me to be his tutor and help him I had to register to get my master's degree too. So here I was working on my master's degree. A high school drop out was now working on her master's degree. My husband and I took a lot of the same classes, so I was able to help him even more. And there were occasions when I sat in his classes to take notes and help him. It was a neat position because I got paid for it. Once again I had my own money. I loved it. And by the time it was over I had another degree to place under my belt.

>>>>>>>>>>>>>>>>>>>>>NOTES>>>>>>>>>>>>>>>>>>>>>>

Chapter Sixteen

Let's talk about money again. The need and want and desire to have my own money, so I dream of numbers and play the lottery. One would ask, is it wrong to play the lottery. if you want to have money,then how do you plan on getting it. One way is to play the lottery and hope for the best. One of my set of numbers did come out. When 123 straight and box 321 I was excited but I had not played it. Why had I not played it. I had not played it because I did not have any money to play it. That's why I am trying to have my own money. Besides I cannot depend on a man to give me money. If I did that then I would not have any money. The bible says that the love of money is the root of all evil. So one is not suppose to love money. But money solves a lot of problems. Money pays for a lot of things. Having money solves a lot of problems. That is why people both men and women will do anything for money. Why do I want to win the lottery? I want to win the lottery so that I can have my own money. Why do I want my own money? I want my own money so that I can spend it on myself. I want to buy myself clothing, shoes, a car, a house, furniture, and all the necessities of life. I also want money so that I can pay off my debts. And I want money so that I can give money away to good causes. I also want to build a foundation. A foundation that donates money to worthy causes. It's not easy to win and earn your own money.

>>>>>>>>>>>>>>>>>>>>>>>NOTES>>>>>>>>>>>>>>>>>>>>>>>

Chapter Seventeen

This is just something I thought I would place in the book for good measure. It's free! I live in an apartment complex even though I want my own house. I prefer my neighbors not to be too close. Apartment neighbors make too much noise. There are children every where. There is noise every where. And of course there is an officer manager to deal with. Even if I do not want to. You would think that Cicely would be for her clients, but that is not the case. When we, that is my mom and I moved talked to Carrie about this apartment, we asked her if you could have a day care and she said yes. As a result we rented a three bedroom. Well when I drew up some posters and put them around in the neighborhood I got a phone call from Cicely. Cicely said that I could not have a business at the apartment complex. I wanted to choke her, because I knew what Carrie had said and if we did not think that we had permission to keep kids we would have never like I said before rented a three bedroom. So, Cicely spent about 15 minutes telling me how I could not have a business in the apartment because she did not want unknown people coming into the complex. And that was so funny hearing that when the gate was down for more than a month and anybody could have and did enter the complex during the day and at night. But Cicely did not want unknown people coming into the complex. What a contradiction! Now more currently, I am trying to sell Avon and Cicely is trying to tell me I cannot do that either. She is also telling me that i have to report that income to the office. Like I am going to make a lot of money selling Avon. You would think that people like Cicely would try to help her residents succeed in what they were trying to do, but that is not the case. Cicely is nasty, bossy and does not like her clients. She has a nasty attitude and does not know how to talk to her clients. She needs to be reported to her bosses. This woman wants to be a boss, but is she really suited to lead?

>>>>>>>>>>>>>>>>>>>>>>>NOTES>>>>>>>>>>>>>>>>>>>>>>>

Chapter Eighteen

As a mom you want your children to be safe. When my daughter was in Afghanistan I was worried about her safety and security. I was worried because of the bombing that was taking place over there. I was worried because of the reports of soldiers loosing their lives. I was scared for her. I just wanted her to be safe. I just wanted her to come home. I nearly went crazy because I was worried about her. I blamed everybody, even the military for her being deployed. I went back and hoped and relived the fact that I did not want her to join the military. I did not trust the military. I was scared. I just wanted her to be safe and I felt she could not be safe in a war zone. I use to dream about being in Afghanistan with her. I think I had these dreams because I wanted to make sure she was safe. I sent her boxes every month to make sure she felt that I loved her. I also wanted her to read about the news back home, so I sent her current magazines. I also sent her snacks and fitness books. How can you send your daughter fitness books and snacks at the same time. Seemed like a contradiction, but I sent her what I thought she would like and some things that she requested. I cannot say in words how hard it was for me toward the end of her term oversees. I did not think I would make it. I thought I would die. And maybe in a way I did. I stopped going to church. I stayed home. I think I blamed God the Father for my dilemma and/or sickness. I did not know what to do. I was scared to go outside. I was scared to drive. I was just scared of everything. But I wanted to live and live I did! And she came home safe and sound. And now she is publishing her new poem book. Poems she had written when she was in high school. Poems that she wrote about herself and her family. I want her book to sale because she is multi-talented and besides I am sure she and I can use the money from the book sales.

>>>>>>>>>>>>>>>>>>>>>>NOTES>>>>>>>>>>>>>>>>>>>>>>>

Chapter Nineteen

I know this little girl that wanted to be loved but was not. Megan needed to be loved by her grandmother, but her grandmother did not like girls. Megan knew how to cook. Meagan knew how to clean. Megan even knew how to go to the grocery store, shop and come home with the food and the money. Megan's grandmother taught her those things, but Megan did not feel loved. If Megan did something wrong, her grandmother would hit her with whatever she had her hand on. One time she hit Megan in the head with a cabbage. And then one time she hit Megan in the head with a construction helmet. Megan remembers the blood spilling down her face and neck. Megan still has the mark in her head still today. Megan could not understand why her grandmother was so mean. It could have been because she was in pain all the time. Agnes attempted to jump from a ledge onto a boat and slipped and fell. From that day she had a injury to her leg. I believe the doctors wanted to cut her leg off but she would not let them do it. She put some ointment on her open scare and covered it with the herbal healing leaves and wrapped it up. The leg would hurt her so much. She was constantly in pain. Agnes would take some powdered medicine and a coke drink back then. That would seem to ease the pain. Agnes ended up dying alone with her dogs. And her dogs had started eating her.

Agnes's grandson did not have to do anything. he did not even have to go to school. He slept all day and then went outside to play. He did not have any chores. He was a boy, so he was highly favored. Agnes saved money for him to go to school. So he went away to college, but it seems that when he left her she began to get worse.

Megan left her grandmother before her brother did. Megan ran away. Megan saved her lunch money and got on the bus and went to her mother's house where she waited at a neighbor's house until her mother came home. Megan's mother was working at the school in the neighborhood. Megan's mother was so glad to see her when she came home. Megan's life would change. She was just twelve years old. She had growed up too soon. She was never a child. Megan knew all of the grownup things to do. Her mother could leave her home with her younger siblings and she would take care of them. She would cook for them and feed them. I remember one time when Megan's mother went to the Bahamas. She left Megan in charge. Megan had the money she left her. She only spent it when needed. Megan did a great job.

>>>>>>>>>>>>>>>>>>>>>>NOTES>>>>>>>>>>>>>>>>>>>>>>>

Chapter Twenty

I thought I was finished with this piece but there is something else I have to say. There is something that I have learned about a woman in the last couple of days. I just could not let this book be published without discussing what I finally realized about a woman. I believe this information is going to help a man. I met this lady and she started telling me all her business. I found out that she was leaving her kids home alone at night while she worked. A twelve year old was taking care of a one year old toddler. I was very concern for the safety of the kids, so I offered my services for pennies because I wanted to help. I told the mother that she could pay me to keep her kids whatever she could afford. And she agreed to let me keep the kids, so I did. Then she decided that she would have their dad check in with them to make sure they were okay and she did not need me. Then about two days later she called me and ask me to keep the kids. I said okay and went right over. She told me she would give me the pass word for the computer, so I brought my lap top with me. I thought it was okay. At 3:30 I received a phone call from my niece's school. She my niece had to be picked up from school. So, I told the little girl I was keeping that I was going to pick someone up and I would be right back. Well about 10 minutes later I received a phone call from her mom saying that I needed to return back to the house and pick up my computer and Avon bag and leave. She fused me out for leaving the house and going right across the street to pick up my niece. Granted maybe I should have called her nd told her I was leaving the house, but I figured this woman is at work and I will be right back, so why do I need to disturb her at work. Plus, she left her kids for months at a time eight hours or longer without any supervision and I was only gone for maybe twenty minutes if that long and she jumped all over me. I was shocked at her reaction. I did not know who I was talking to. Remember now this woman approached me and started talking to me. I was not trying to meet her or hold a conversation with her. I was not trying to know her business. But I did cause she did, so I felt like I needed to do something to help her. That was my motive. I was concerned for the safety and the well being of her kids. I gave them my heart and it cost me.

This lesson taught me something that I knew about women. Some women need and want you to help them. They are always in need of some help. And then when you help them they criticize you for being so stupid as to help them. And its all because they want to be in control. From my experience there are women who want to help you especially if they think you have potential. And the assistance and help they give you does not cost you anything.

I would rather work with a bunch of men than to have anything to do with a bunch of women. The reason why women do not rule the world is because they cannot get together, they are constantly bickering and fighting among themselves. Women are jealous of one another and do not want to see one woman get ahead of another. All in the name of being in control. Maybe the answer is to give up some of the control issues that women have in order to succeed. I think some women understand that dilemma, but some women have not gotten it yet. But they will!

>>>>>>>>>>>>>>>>>>>>>>NOTES>>>>>>>>>>>>>>>>>>>>>>

www.ingramcontent.com/pod-product-compliance
Lightning Source LLC
Chambersburg PA
CBHW020356290526
45785CB00005B/2310